Peter Pomerantsev

Once upon a time, in the heart of the Soviet Union's final years, Pyotr Igorevich Pomerantsev was born into a family that would shape his destiny amidst the tumultuous landscape of post-Soviet Russia. Born in 1977 in Kyiv, Ukraine, young Pyotr's journey began against the backdrop of a nation in flux.

His parents, Igor and Liana Pomerantsev, were no ordinary couple. Igor, a broadcaster and poet, dared to challenge the oppressive regime of the Soviet era, distributing anti-Soviet literature that caught the watchful eye of the KGB. Fearing for their safety, the family fled to the West, seeking refuge in the vibrant streets of Munich, Germany, before finally settling in the eclectic city of London, where the BBC World Service provided sanctuary for Igor's talents.

In the bustling cultural mosaic of London, Peter, as he came to be known, found his footing. Amidst the rich tapestry of his upbringing, with a father dedicated to truth and a mother who excelled in documentary production, Peter's passion for storytelling was ignited.

He pursued his education with vigor, attending Westminster School in London and the European School in Munich. Fuelled by a curiosity for languages and literature, he embarked on a journey of intellectual exploration at the University of Edinburgh, delving into the realms of English Literature and German.

But it was Russia, the land of his birth, that beckoned to him with an irresistible allure. In 2001, armed with a thirst for adventure and a desire to uncover the truth behind the enigmatic facade of post-Soviet society, Peter made his way to Moscow.

In the pulsating heart of the Russian capital, Peter immersed himself in the world of television, crafting narratives that danced on the edges of reality. From his perch at Russian entertainment channel TNT, he wove tales that captivated audiences, all the while navigating the intricate web of political intrigue that defined Putin's Russia.

Yet, Peter's journey was not confined to the realm of television. With a pen as his sword, he ventured into the realm of journalism, fearlessly exposing the machinations of power and the murky depths of propaganda. Through his articles in esteemed publications like Newsweek and The Atlantic Monthly, he coined the term "post-modern dictatorship," offering a piercing insight into the surreal landscape of contemporary Russia.

His magnum opus, "Nothing Is True and Everything Is Possible: Adventures in Modern Russia," unveiled the dark underbelly of Putin's regime, earning accolades and acclaim from critics and readers alike. With each word penned, Peter peeled back the layers of deception, revealing a world where truth was but a fleeting illusion.

As his reputation grew, Peter became a beacon of truth in a world shrouded in lies. From the hallowed halls of academia to the corridors of power, he lent his voice to the fight against disinformation, testifying before the US Congress and the UK Parliament with a fervor born of conviction.

After his university years, Peter felt drawn to the enigmatic allure of Russia, the land of his birth. In 2001, he ventured into the heart of Moscow, a city pulsating with energy and contradictions. Immersed in the cacophony of post-Soviet Russia, Peter found himself captivated by the fusion of chaos and creativity that defined the nation's zeitgeist.

His foray into the world of television production became a gateway to understanding the intricacies of Russian society. From his perch in Moscow, Peter witnessed firsthand the evolution of Russian media, navigating the labyrinthine landscape of propaganda and disinformation that pervaded the airwaves.

Intrigued by the power of storytelling to shape perceptions and manipulate reality, Peter embarked on a new chapter in his career as a journalist. With a keen eye for detail and a fearless determination to uncover the truth, he delved deep into the shadows of Russian politics, shining a light on the dark underbelly of the post-modern dictatorship that Vladimir Putin had constructed.

His seminal work, "Nothing Is True and Everything Is Possible: Adventures in Modern Russia," laid bare the surreal heart of the new Russia, revealing a world where truth was subjective and reality was a mere illusion. Transcending borders and languages, Peter's words resonated with readers around the globe, sparking a dialogue on the nature of power and the fragility of truth in an age of information warfare.

But Peter's quest for truth extended beyond the confines of journalism. As a Senior Fellow at the London School of Economics, he sought to understand the mechanisms of propaganda and disinformation that threatened to undermine the very fabric of democratic societies.

With each passing year, Peter's voice grew louder, his influence reaching new heights as he testified before the halls of power in Washington and London. From the corridors of academia to the front lines of the information war, Peter Pomerantsev emerged as a steadfast champion of truth and transparency in an age of uncertainty.

Yet amidst the chaos of his professional life, Peter found solace and joy in the embrace of his family. With his Russian wife by his side and their children growing up in the vibrant metropolis of London, Peter discovered that the greatest stories were often found not in the headlines of newspapers, but in the quiet moments shared with loved ones.

As the pages of his life continued to unfold, Peter Pomerantsev remained steadfast in his commitment to unraveling the mysteries of our world, one story at a time. And though the road ahead may be fraught with challenges and uncertainties, Peter faced the future with unwavering courage and an indomitable spirit, knowing that the power of truth would always prevail in the end.

As Peter's reputation as a voice of reason and insight grew, so did his dedication to understanding the intricate web of modern politics and media manipulation. His work transcended the boundaries of traditional journalism, leading him to explore the depths of information warfare and propaganda, unearthing truths hidden beneath layers of deception.

With each passing year, Peter's influence expanded, his insights sought after by policymakers and scholars alike. From testifying before congressional committees to collaborating with international think tanks, he became a beacon of clarity in a world mired in confusion.

Yet, amidst the whirlwind of his professional endeavors, Peter remained grounded by his personal connections. His family, with whom he shared the joys and challenges of life, provided him with strength and purpose. His wife, a constant source of support and inspiration, stood by his side as he navigated the complexities of his career.

As his children grew, Peter found himself reflecting on the world he was shaping for future generations. With each new book and article, he sought to illuminate the path forward, offering insights into the forces that shape our society and the power of individuals to effect change.

But Peter's journey was far from over. With each new project, each new endeavor, he continued to push the boundaries of knowledge and understanding, determined to leave a lasting impact on the world around him.

And so, as the sun set on another chapter in Peter Pomerantsev's remarkable life, he looked towards the horizon with anticipation and hope, knowing that the road ahead would be filled with challenges and opportunities. But with courage in his heart and truth as his guiding light, he was ready to face whatever the future held, confident in his ability to make a difference in the world.

In the ever-evolving landscape of global affairs, Peter Pomerantsev remained a steadfast figure, committed to shedding light on the shadows of misinformation and disinformation. His relentless pursuit of truth took him to the far corners of the world, from the corridors of power in Washington to the bustling streets of Moscow, where he continued to unravel the mysteries of modern politics and media manipulation.

With each passing year, Peter's voice grew stronger, resonating with audiences around the world who sought clarity amidst the chaos of the information age. His books became essential reading for policymakers, journalists, and scholars alike, offering invaluable insights into the inner workings of authoritarian regimes and the fragility of democratic societies.

But Peter's impact extended beyond the realm of academia and journalism. As a devoted husband and father, he found fulfillment in the simple pleasures of family life, cherishing the moments spent with his loved ones amidst the hectic pace of his career.

As the years went by, Peter's legacy continued to grow, his contributions to the field of global affairs leaving an indelible mark on the world. Yet, amidst the accolades and achievements, he remained humble, ever mindful of the responsibility that came with his platform.

For Peter Pomerantsev, the journey was far from over. With each new challenge, each new opportunity, he embraced the unknown with courage and conviction, knowing that the pursuit of truth was a lifelong endeavor worth fighting for.

And so, as the pages of his life turned, Peter Pomerantsev stood as a beacon of hope in a world beset by uncertainty, his unwavering commitment to truth and transparency serving as a guiding light for generations to come.

As the years unfolded, Peter Pomerantsev's passion for truth and his commitment to shedding light on the complexities of the modern world only deepened. With each new project, each new revelation, he continued to make his mark on the global stage, earning accolades and recognition for his tireless efforts.

His exploration into the depths of information warfare and propaganda took him to new heights of understanding, as he dissected the mechanisms by which truth could be twisted and reality distorted. From the halls of academia to the corridors of power, Peter's voice resonated with clarity and conviction, challenging conventional wisdom and inspiring change.

But amidst the chaos of his professional life, Peter always found solace in the quiet moments spent with his family. His wife, a steadfast partner in his journey, and his children, a source of boundless joy and inspiration, grounded him in the midst of uncertainty.

As he looked back on his life's work, Peter felt a profound sense of gratitude for the experiences that had shaped him and the people who had supported him along the way. From his upbringing in the tumultuous days of post-Soviet Russia to his current role as a respected voice in global affairs, he had come full circle, guided by a steadfast commitment to truth and integrity.

And so, as the sun set on another chapter in Peter Pomerantsev's extraordinary life, he knew that the journey was far from over. With each new day came new challenges to confront and new opportunities to seize. But armed with the wisdom of experience and the courage of conviction, he faced the future with unwavering resolve, ready to continue his quest for truth in a world hungry for understanding.

As Peter Pomerantsev stepped into the next chapter of his life, the world around him seemed to shift and change with a rapidity that matched the pace of his own evolution. His work had taken on a new urgency, a sense of purpose that drove him to delve deeper into the complexities of modern society.

With each passing year, Peter's insights grew sharper, his understanding of the forces at play in the world more profound. He continued to write and speak, sharing his knowledge and perspective with a growing audience eager for clarity in an age of confusion.

But as much as he thrived in the public sphere, Peter remained grounded in his personal life. His family, now grown and flourishing, remained the bedrock of his existence. His wife, his children, and his extended family provided him with the love and support he needed to face the challenges of his work with courage and determination.

As he looked towards the future, Peter knew that there were still battles to be fought and truths to be uncovered. But he faced the unknown with a sense of optimism, knowing that his journey had only just begun and that the road ahead was filled with endless possibilities.

And so, Peter Pomerantsev continued on his quest for truth, a modern-day explorer navigating the murky waters of disinformation and propaganda, guided by his unwavering commitment to uncovering the truth and sharing it with the world.

As Peter Pomerantsev continued on his quest for truth, his journey took him to new and unexpected places, both geographically and intellectually. With each step forward, he encountered new challenges and opportunities, pushing the boundaries of his understanding and expanding the scope of his work.

From the bustling streets of Moscow to the halls of power in Washington, D.C., Peter's voice reverberated with clarity and conviction, drawing attention to the pressing issues of our time. His tireless advocacy for transparency and accountability earned him respect and admiration from colleagues and adversaries alike, cementing his reputation as a leading authority on the intersection of media, politics, and power.

But amidst the chaos of his professional life, Peter never lost sight of what mattered most: his family. His wife and children remained his anchor, providing him with unwavering support and unconditional love as he navigated the complexities of his work.

As he reflected on the path that had led him to this moment, Peter felt a profound sense of gratitude for the opportunities he had been given and the people who had helped him along the way. With each passing day, he was reminded of the immense responsibility that came with his platform, a responsibility he embraced wholeheartedly, knowing that the work he was doing was more important now than ever before.

And so, as Peter Pomerantsev looked towards the future, he did so with a sense of purpose and determination, ready to confront whatever challenges lay ahead with courage and resilience. For him, the quest for truth was not just a profession, but a calling—a calling he would continue to answer with unwavering dedication for years to come.

As Peter Pomerantsev forged ahead on his journey, he found himself increasingly drawn to the forefront of global conversations on disinformation and propaganda. His insights became sought after by world leaders and policymakers, his voice a beacon of clarity in a sea of confusion.

But amidst the accolades and recognition, Peter remained grounded by his roots and his values. He never forgot the sacrifices his family had made for him, nor the lessons he had learned from his upbringing in the shadow of the Soviet Union. These experiences fueled his determination to expose falsehoods and champion the truth, no matter the cost.

As the world grappled with the ever-evolving landscape of media manipulation and political intrigue, Peter saw his work take on new significance. His writings and speeches resonated with audiences around the globe, inspiring others to join him in the fight for transparency and accountability.

But for Peter, the true measure of success lay not in awards or accolades, but in the impact he was able to have on the world around him. Whether through his writing, his speaking engagements, or his advocacy work, he remained committed to making a difference in the lives of others.

And so, as Peter Pomerantsev continued to chart his course through the tumult of the modern world, he did so with a sense of purpose and determination. For him, the quest for truth was not just a professional pursuit, but a moral imperative—a calling he would continue to answer with unwavering resolve for as long as he lived.

With each passing day, Peter Pomerantsev felt the weight of responsibility resting heavily on his shoulders. The world looked to him for guidance, for insight, for a way forward in an increasingly complex and uncertain landscape. And he did not take this responsibility lightly.

Drawing on the wisdom gained from his experiences and the lessons learned from his family, Peter forged ahead with unwavering determination. He knew that the work he was doing was more important than ever before, that the truths he uncovered had the power to shape the course of history.

But amidst the chaos of his professional life, Peter always made time for what truly mattered: his loved ones. His wife, his children, his parents—they were his rock, his anchor in the storm. They reminded him of the values he held dear, of the reasons why he had embarked on this journey in the first place.

And so, as Peter Pomerantsev continued to navigate the twists and turns of his remarkable life, he did so with humility and grace. For him, the pursuit of truth was not just a lofty ideal, but a deeply personal mission—a mission he would pursue with unwavering passion and unwavering commitment until his last breath.

In the quiet moments of reflection, Peter Pomerantsev often found himself pondering the profound impact of his work and the legacy he hoped to leave behind. With each word penned and each speech delivered, he sought not only to inform but to inspire, to ignite a spark of curiosity and critical thinking in the hearts and minds of his audience.

As he delved deeper into the intricacies of media manipulation and political propaganda, Peter remained acutely aware of the immense responsibility that came with his platform. He understood that the truths he uncovered had the power to shape public discourse, to influence the decisions of policymakers, and to safeguard the foundations of democracy itself.

But amidst the weighty expectations placed upon him, Peter never lost sight of his humanity. He cherished the moments spent with his family, relishing in the laughter of his children and the comfort of his wife's embrace. They were his refuge, his sanctuary in a world fraught with uncertainty.

And so, armed with the love and support of his family and fueled by an unwavering commitment to truth and integrity, Peter Pomerantsev faced the future with courage and conviction. For him, the journey was far from over, and the quest for truth would continue to guide his path, illuminating the darkness and inspiring hope in the hearts of all who crossed his path.

In the quiet hours of the night, when the world outside seemed to slow its frenetic pace, Peter Pomerantsev often found himself lost in thought. He pondered the complexities of the human condition, the tangled web of truth and deception that wove its way through every aspect of society.

With each passing day, the weight of his responsibilities grew heavier, as did the urgency of his mission. But amidst the chaos of his professional life, Peter drew strength from the unwavering support of his family. They were his rock, his guiding light in a world filled with uncertainty.

As he delved deeper into the dark heart of disinformation and propaganda, Peter remained steadfast in his commitment to uncovering the truth. He knew that the path ahead would be fraught with challenges and obstacles, but he was undeterred.

For Peter Pomerantsev, the pursuit of truth was not just a career—it was a calling, a sacred duty that he would continue to uphold with unwavering dedication. And as he looked towards the horizon, he knew that his journey was far from over. With each step forward, he moved closer to the elusive truth that lay at the heart of it all.

As the dawn broke over the horizon, casting its gentle light upon the world, Peter Pomerantsev felt a renewed sense of purpose stirring within him. The challenges ahead loomed large, but he faced them with a quiet resolve, knowing that his mission was more vital now than ever before.

With each word he wrote and each speech he delivered, Peter sought to pierce through the veil of deception that shrouded society, to shine a light on the darkest corners of human nature. He understood that the truth was a fragile thing, easily obscured by the machinations of those who sought to manipulate it for their own gain.

But amidst the chaos and confusion, Peter found solace in the love of his family. They were his sanctuary, his refuge from the storm. Their unwavering support sustained him through the long hours and sleepless nights, reminding him of the importance of the work he was doing.

As he set out to face the challenges of the day, Peter carried with him the wisdom of generations past and the hope of generations yet to come. For him, the pursuit of truth was not just a noble ideal—it was a fundamental principle upon which the future of humanity depended.

And so, with a steady hand and a determined spirit, Peter Pomerantsev ventured forth into the unknown, ready to confront whatever trials lay ahead. For in the end, he knew that the truth would prevail, and that his efforts would not be in vain.

With each step forward, Peter Pomerantsev felt the weight of his purpose pressing down upon him, urging him onward in his quest for truth. He knew that the road ahead would be fraught with challenges and obstacles, but he faced them with a steely resolve born of conviction and dedication.

As he traversed the ever-shifting landscape of media manipulation and political intrigue, Peter remained guided by the values instilled in him by his family and upbringing. Their unwavering support served as a constant reminder of the importance of his mission, spurring him on even in the darkest of times.

With each passing day, Peter's resolve only grew stronger, his determination unyielding in the face of adversity. He understood that the pursuit of truth was not for the faint of heart, but he embraced the challenge wholeheartedly, knowing that the stakes were too high to do otherwise.

And so, as he continued to navigate the complexities of his work, Peter Pomerantsev did so with a sense of purpose and clarity that few could match. For him, the quest for truth was not just a professional endeavor, but a deeply personal journey—a journey that he would continue to pursue with unwavering determination for as long as he lived.

With each passing moment, Peter Pomerantsev felt the gravity of his calling pulling him deeper into the labyrinth of truth and deceit. The world around him seemed to pulse with an energy all its own, a palpable tension that spoke to the urgency of his mission.

As he delved ever deeper into the shadows, Peter found himself confronting uncomfortable truths and unsettling realities. Yet, he pressed on undeterred, driven by a relentless determination to expose the lies and distortions that threatened to undermine the very fabric of society.

But amidst the chaos and confusion, Peter found solace in the unwavering support of his loved ones. His family stood by him, a bastion of strength and stability in a world gone mad. Their love and encouragement fueled his spirit, propelling him forward even when the darkness threatened to consume him.

And so, with courage in his heart and truth as his guide, Peter Pomerantsev forged ahead into the unknown. For he knew that the quest for truth was not just a journey—it was a battle, a battle that he was determined to win at any cost. And win it he would, for the sake of all those who depended on him, and for the future of a world in desperate need of clarity and understanding.

With each step he took, Peter Pomerantsev felt the weight of responsibility bearing down on him like a heavy cloak. The path ahead was fraught with uncertainty, yet he walked it with unwavering determination, fueled by a burning desire to uncover the truth and expose the lies that threatened to tear society apart.

As he journeyed deeper into the heart of darkness, Peter found himself confronting the demons that lurked within. The walls of deceit closed in around him, threatening to suffocate him with their suffocating grasp. Yet, he refused to be silenced, his voice ringing out like a beacon of hope in the night.

But amidst the chaos and turmoil, Peter found solace in the love of his family. Their unwavering support buoyed his spirits, reminding him of the purpose behind his quest and the importance of the work he was doing.

And so, with courage in his heart and fire in his soul, Peter Pomerantsev pressed on, determined to shine a light in the darkness and illuminate the path to a better tomorrow. For he knew that the fight for truth was not just his own—it was a battle that must be fought by all who cherished freedom and justice. And he would not rest until victory was won, no matter the cost.

With each passing day, Peter Pomerantsev felt the weight of his mission growing heavier upon his shoulders. The world seemed to be teetering on the brink of chaos, with truth becoming an ever more elusive commodity. Yet, in the face of such daunting odds, Peter refused to waver.

As he delved deeper into the labyrinth of disinformation and propaganda, Peter found himself confronting the very essence of human nature. He saw the power of manipulation at work, twisting minds and distorting reality with ease. But he also witnessed the resilience of the human spirit, the unwavering determination of those who refused to be deceived.

But amidst the turmoil of his professional life, Peter found solace in the quiet moments spent with his family. Their love and support served as a beacon of hope in a world filled with darkness, reminding him of the values that guided him on his journey.

And so, with each new revelation and each new challenge, Peter Pomerantsev pressed on, fueled by a sense of purpose and a commitment to truth that burned brighter than ever before. For he knew that the fight for truth was not just a battle—it was a crusade, a crusade that he would continue to wage with unwavering resolve until the very end.

With each passing challenge, Peter Pomerantsev felt his resolve strengthen, his determination solidify into an unbreakable force. The world around him seemed to tremble under the weight of deception, but Peter stood firm, a bastion of truth in a sea of lies.

As he delved deeper into the heart of darkness, Peter uncovered layers upon layers of deceit, each revelation fueling his determination to expose the truth. He refused to be swayed by the temptations of complacency or the allure of ignorance, knowing that the fight for truth demanded his unwavering commitment.

But amidst the chaos and confusion, Peter found moments of clarity and peace in the embrace of his family. Their love and support fortified him, grounding him in the knowledge that he was not alone in his quest.

And so, with courage in his heart and truth as his shield, Peter Pomerantsev continued to march forward, undeterred by the obstacles that lay ahead. For he knew that the pursuit of truth was not just a noble endeavor—it was a sacred duty, one that he would fulfill with every fiber of his being, for as long as it took to prevail.

With each step forward, Peter Pomerantsev felt the weight of responsibility pressing down upon him, urging him onward in his quest for truth. The world around him seemed to pulse with an energy all its own, a palpable tension that spoke to the urgency of his mission.

As he delved ever deeper into the shadows, Peter found himself confronting uncomfortable truths and unsettling realities. Yet, he pressed on undeterred, driven by a relentless determination to expose the lies and distortions that threatened to undermine the very fabric of society.

But amidst the chaos and confusion, Peter found solace in the unwavering support of his loved ones. His family stood by him, a bastion of strength and stability in a world gone mad. Their love and encouragement fueled his spirit, propelling him forward even when the darkness threatened to consume him.

And so, with courage in his heart and truth as his guide, Peter Pomerantsev forged ahead into the unknown. For he knew that the quest for truth was not just a journey—it was a battle, a battle that he was determined to win at any cost. And win it he would, for the sake of all those who depended on him, and for the future of a world in desperate need of clarity and understanding.

As the dawn broke over the horizon, casting its gentle light upon the world, Peter Pomerantsev felt a renewed sense of purpose stirring within him. The challenges ahead loomed large, but he faced them with a quiet resolve, knowing that his mission was more vital now than ever before.

With each word he wrote and each speech he delivered, Peter sought to pierce through the veil of deception that shrouded society, to shine a light on the darkest corners of human nature. He understood that the truth was a fragile thing, easily obscured by the machinations of those who sought to manipulate it for their own gain.

But amidst the chaos and turmoil, Peter found solace in the love of his family. Their unwavering support buoyed his spirits, reminding him of the purpose behind his quest and the importance of the work he was doing.

As he set out to face the challenges of the day, Peter carried with him the wisdom of generations past and the hope of generations yet to come. For him, the pursuit of truth was not just a noble ideal—it was a fundamental principle upon which the future of humanity depended.

And so, with a steady hand and a determined spirit, Peter Pomerantsev ventured forth into the unknown, ready to confront whatever trials lay ahead. For in the end, he knew that the truth would prevail, and that his efforts would not be in vain.

With each step he took, Peter Pomerantsev felt the weight of responsibility bearing down on him like a heavy cloak. The path ahead was fraught with uncertainty, yet he walked it with unwavering determination, fueled by a burning desire to uncover the truth and expose the lies that threatened to tear society apart.

As he journeyed deeper into the heart of darkness, Peter found himself confronting the very essence of human nature. He saw the power of manipulation at work, twisting minds and distorting reality with ease. But he also witnessed the resilience of the human spirit, the unwavering determination of those who refused to be deceived.

But amidst the turmoil of his professional life, Peter found solace in the quiet moments spent with his family. Their love and support served as a beacon of hope in a world filled with darkness, reminding him of the values that guided him on his journey.

And so, with each new revelation and each new challenge, Peter Pomerantsev pressed on, fueled by a sense of purpose and a commitment to truth that burned brighter than ever before. For he knew that the fight for truth was not just a battle—it was a crusade, a crusade that he would continue to wage with unwavering resolve until the very end.

With the weight of truth on his shoulders and the support of his loved ones in his heart, Peter Pomerantsev faced the daunting task ahead with unwavering determination. He understood that the journey to uncovering truth was not a solitary one, but a collective effort that required courage, resilience, and unwavering dedication.

As he ventured further into the depths of deception, Peter encountered challenges that tested his resolve and adversaries who sought to thwart his mission. Yet, he refused to be deterred, drawing strength from the knowledge that he carried with him the hopes and aspirations of those who yearned for a world built on honesty and integrity.

In moments of doubt, Peter found solace in the memories of his upbringing, the lessons imparted by his family, and the wisdom gained from his experiences. These anchors kept him grounded amidst the tumult of his journey, reminding him of the principles that guided his pursuit of truth.

With each obstacle overcome and each revelation uncovered, Peter Pomerantsev moved closer to his ultimate goal. He knew that the road ahead would be fraught with challenges, but he faced it with a steely resolve, knowing that the pursuit of truth was not just a mission—it was a calling, one that he embraced with every fiber of his being.

With unwavering determination and a steadfast commitment to his mission, Peter Pomerantsev continued to navigate the treacherous waters of deception and manipulation. Every step forward brought him closer to the elusive truth he sought, but also deeper into the shadows where falsehoods lurked.

Yet, Peter was undeterred. His resolve remained unshakeable, fueled by the knowledge that his efforts were not in vain. For with each revelation, he uncovered a piece of the puzzle, shining a light into the darkest corners of society and exposing the lies that threatened to undermine it.

As he delved deeper into his investigation, Peter encountered resistance from those who sought to silence him, to obscure the truth and maintain their grip on power. But he refused to be silenced, his voice growing stronger with each attempt to silence it.

In moments of doubt, Peter drew strength from the unwavering support of his family and the countless individuals who stood behind him. Their belief in his mission fueled his determination, propelling him forward even in the face of adversity.

And so, with courage in his heart and truth as his guide, Peter Pomerantsev continued to fight the good fight, knowing that the pursuit of truth was not just a noble endeavor—it was a fundamental necessity for the preservation of democracy and the protection of human rights. And he would not rest until justice prevailed and truth triumphed over deception.

With each passing day, Peter Pomerantsev felt the weight of his mission pressing down on him, urging him to push forward despite the obstacles in his path. The road ahead was fraught with danger and uncertainty, but he knew that he could not falter in his pursuit of truth.

As he delved deeper into the murky depths of deception, Peter uncovered layer upon layer of lies and manipulation. Yet, for every falsehood he exposed, it seemed that two more sprang up in its place. The task before him seemed daunting, but Peter refused to be daunted.

With each setback, he found renewed determination to press on, fueled by the knowledge that the truth was worth fighting for. He drew strength from the support of his loved ones, who stood by him unwaveringly in his quest for justice.

And so, with his resolve steeled and his spirit unbroken, Peter Pomerantsev continued to march forward, undeterred by the challenges that lay ahead. For he knew that the pursuit of truth was not just a personal mission—it was a duty he owed to society, to ensure that the light of truth continued to shine brightly in a world too often shrouded in darkness.

In the face of mounting challenges, Peter Pomerantsev's dedication to exposing the intricate web of misinformation grew only stronger. His investigations took him to the furthest reaches of the digital world, where the lines between reality and fabrication blurred, and the shadows of influence extended far beyond what the eye could see.

Peter's work was more than just an investigation; it was a journey into the heart of darkness, where the battle for the soul of information waged fiercely. Yet, his resolve never wavered. With each piece of the puzzle that he put into place, the bigger picture began to emerge, revealing the scale and complexity of the disinformation campaigns that sought to manipulate public opinion and undermine democratic institutions.

Amidst the noise and chaos, Peter's voice emerged as a beacon of clarity and reason. His writings and public appearances became rallying points for those who valued truth and integrity. Through his efforts, he helped to foster a greater awareness of the threats posed by disinformation and the importance of media literacy in safeguarding democracy.

As the world grappled with the implications of his findings, Peter remained committed to his cause. He understood that the fight against misinformation was not one that could be won overnight. It required vigilance, resilience, and a collective effort to champion the truth.

With the unwavering support of his family and the global community that had come to recognize the importance of his work, Peter Pomerantsev pressed on. His journey was a testament to the power of one individual's commitment to truth and justice, serving as an inspiration to all who believe in the fundamental right to factual and transparent information.

In this ever-evolving battle between truth and falsehood, Peter stood as a steadfast guardian of reality, armed with the unyielding power of his convictions and the unbreakable spirit of hope. The road ahead remained uncertain, but one thing was clear: as long as there were voices like Peter's, willing to speak out and stand up for truth, the darkness of disinformation would never prevail.

With every keystroke and every word spoken, Peter Pomerantsev advanced further into the heart of the disinformation battlefield. Each revelation he unearthed added another layer of complexity to the intricate tapestry of deceit woven by those seeking to manipulate the truth.

Yet, Peter's determination remained unshaken. He understood that the fight against disinformation was not merely about exposing lies—it was about empowering individuals to discern fact from fiction, to question narratives, and to demand transparency from those in positions of power.

As he delved deeper into his investigations, Peter encountered resistance from those vested in maintaining the status quo. But he refused to be silenced or deterred. He knew that the stakes were too high, that the very fabric of democracy hung in the balance.

Supported by a network of allies and advocates who shared his commitment to truth, Peter pressed on. He knew that he was not alone in his mission, that there were countless others who stood ready to join him in the fight against misinformation and propaganda.

And so, with each passing day, Peter Pomerantsev continued to march forward, his resolve unwavering, his spirit indomitable. For he knew that the pursuit of truth was not just a battle—it was a moral imperative, one that demanded nothing less than his full dedication and unwavering resolve. And he would not rest until the light of truth shone bright, illuminating the darkness of deception and falsehood for all to see.

As Peter Pomerantsev delved deeper into the labyrinth of disinformation, he found himself confronting the very essence of truth itself. It was a battle fought not just on the digital battlegrounds of social media and online forums, but in the hearts and minds of people around the world.

With each new revelation, Peter uncovered the intricate ways in which misinformation spread like wildfire, shaping public opinion and sowing seeds of doubt and division. But he refused to be daunted by the enormity of the task before him. Instead, he drew strength from the knowledge that the pursuit of truth was a noble endeavor, one worth fighting for at any cost.

As he worked tirelessly to expose the lies and manipulations that threatened to undermine democracy, Peter found solace in the support of his family and colleagues. Their unwavering belief in his mission gave him the strength to carry on, even in the face of seemingly insurmountable odds.

And so, armed with courage, conviction, and a relentless dedication to truth, Peter Pomerantsev forged ahead. His journey was far from over, but he knew that with each battle fought and each victory won, the light of truth grew stronger, shining ever brighter in the darkness of deception. And he would continue to fight until every shadow was banished, and truth reigned supreme once more.

With the weight of truth on his shoulders and the support of his loved ones in his heart, Peter Pomerantsev faced the daunting task ahead with unwavering determination. He understood that the journey to uncovering truth was not a solitary one, but a collective effort that required courage, resilience, and unwavering dedication.

As he ventured further into the depths of deception, Peter encountered challenges that tested his resolve and adversaries who sought to thwart his mission. Yet, he refused to be deterred, drawing strength from the knowledge that he carried with him the hopes and aspirations of those who yearned for a world built on honesty and integrity.

In moments of doubt, Peter found solace in the memories of his upbringing, the lessons imparted by his family, and the wisdom gained from his experiences. These anchors kept him grounded amidst the tumult of his journey, reminding him of the principles that guided his pursuit of truth.

With each obstacle overcome and each revelation uncovered, Peter Pomerantsev moved closer to his ultimate goal. He knew that the road ahead would be fraught with challenges, but he faced it with a steely resolve, knowing that the pursuit of truth was not just a mission—it was a calling, one that he embraced with every fiber of his being.

With each step forward, Peter Pomerantsev felt the weight of responsibility pressing down upon him, urging him onward in his quest for truth. The world around him seemed to pulse with an energy all its own, a palpable tension that spoke to the urgency of his mission.

As he delved ever deeper into the shadows, Peter found himself confronting uncomfortable truths and unsettling realities. Yet, he pressed on undeterred, driven by a relentless determination to expose the lies and distortions that threatened to undermine the very fabric of society.

But amidst the chaos and confusion, Peter found solace in the unwavering support of his loved ones. His family stood by him, a bastion of strength and stability in a world gone mad. Their love and encouragement fueled his spirit, propelling him forward even when the darkness threatened to consume him.

And so, with courage in his heart and truth as his guide, Peter Pomerantsev forged ahead into the unknown. For he knew that the quest for truth was not just a journey—it was a battle, a battle that he was determined to win at any cost. And win it he would, for the sake of all those who depended on him, and for the future of a world in desperate need of clarity and understanding.

With unwavering determination and a steadfast commitment to his mission, Peter Pomerantsev continued to navigate the treacherous waters of deception and manipulation. Every step forward brought him closer to the elusive truth he sought, but also deeper into the shadows where falsehoods lurked.

Yet, Peter was undeterred. His resolve remained unshakeable, fueled by the knowledge that his efforts were not in vain. For with each revelation, he uncovered a piece of the puzzle, shining a light into the darkest corners of society and exposing the lies that threatened to undermine it.

As he delved deeper into his investigation, Peter encountered resistance from those who sought to silence him, to obscure the truth and maintain their grip on power. But he refused to be silenced, his voice growing stronger with each attempt to silence it.

In moments of doubt, Peter drew strength from the unwavering support of his family and the countless individuals who stood behind him. Their belief in his mission fueled his determination, propelling him forward even in the face of adversity.

And so, ith courage in his heart and truth as his shield, Peter Pomerantsev continued to fight the good fight, knowing that the pursuit of truth was not just a noble endeavor—it was a fundamental necessity for the preservation of democracy and the protection of human rights. And he would not rest until justice prevailed and truth triumphed over deception.

In the face of mounting challenges, Peter Pomerantsev's dedication to exposing the intricate web of misinformation grew only stronger. His investigations took him to the furthest reaches of the digital world, where the lines between reality and fabrication blurred, and the shadows of influence extended far beyond what the eye could see.

Peter's work was more than just an investigation; it was a journey into the heart of darkness, where the battle for the soul of information waged fiercely. Yet, his resolve never wavered. With each piece of the puzzle that he put into place, the bigger picture began to emerge, revealing the scale and complexity of the disinformation campaigns that sought to manipulate public opinion and undermine democratic institutions.

Amidst the noise and chaos, Peter's voice emerged as a beacon of clarity and reason. His writings and public appearances became rallying points for those who valued truth and integrity. Through his efforts, he helped to foster a greater awareness of the threats posed by disinformation and the importance of media literacy in safeguarding democracy.

As the world grappled with the implications of his findings, Peter remained committed to his cause. He understood that the fight against misinformation was not one that could be won overnight. It required vigilance, resilience, and a collective effort to champion the truth.

With the unwavering support of his family and the global community that had come to recognize the importance of his work, Peter Pomerantsev pressed on. His journey was a testament to the power of one individual's commitment to truth and justice, serving as an inspiration to all who believe in the fundamental right to factual and transparent information.

In this ever-evolving battle between truth and falsehood, Peter stood as a steadfast guardian of reality, armed with the unyielding power of his convictions and the unbreakable spirit of hope. The road ahead remained uncertain, but one thing was clear: as long as there were voices like Peter's, willing to speak out and stand up for truth, the darkness of disinformation would never prevail.

With every keystroke and every word spoken, Peter Pomerantsev advanced further into the heart of the disinformation battlefield. Each revelation he unearthed added another layer of complexity to the intricate tapestry of deceit woven by those seeking to manipulate the truth.

Yet, Peter's determination remained unshaken. He understood that the fight against disinformation was not merely about exposing lies—it was about empowering individuals to discern fact from fiction, to question narratives, and to demand transparency from those in positions of power.

As he worked tirelessly to expose the lies and manipulations that threatened to undermine democracy, Peter found solace in the support of his family and colleagues. Their unwavering belief in his mission gave him the strength to carry on, even in the face of seemingly insurmountable odds.

And so, armed with courage, conviction, and a relentless dedication to truth, Peter Pomerantsev forged ahead. His journey was far from over, but he knew that with each battle fought and each victory won, the light of truth grew stronger, shining ever brighter in the darkness of deception. And he would continue to fight until every shadow was banished, and truth reigned supreme once more.

With the weight of truth on his shoulders and the support of his loved ones in his heart, Peter Pomerantsev faced the daunting task ahead with unwavering determination. He understood that the journey to uncovering truth was not a solitary one, but a collective effort that required courage, resilience, and unwavering dedication.

As he ventured further into the depths of deception, Peter encountered challenges that tested his resolve and adversaries who sought to thwart his mission. Yet, he refused to be deterred, drawing strength from the knowledge that he carried with him the hopes and aspirations of those who yearned for a world built on honesty and integrity.

In moments of doubt, Peter found solace in the memories of his upbringing, the lessons imparted by his family, and the wisdom gained from his experiences. These anchors kept him grounded amidst the tumult of his journey, reminding him of the principles that guided his pursuit of truth.

With each obstacle overcome and each revelation uncovered, Peter Pomerantsev moved closer to his ultimate goal. He knew that the road ahead would be fraught with challenges, but he faced it with a steely resolve, knowing that the pursuit of truth was not just a mission—it was a calling, one that he embraced with every fiber of his being.

With unwavering determination and a steadfast commitment to his mission, Peter Pomerantsev continued to navigate the treacherous waters of deception and manipulation. Every step forward brought him closer to the elusive truth he sought, but also deeper into the shadows where falsehoods lurked.

Yet, Peter was undeterred. His resolve remained unshakeable, fueled by the knowledge that his efforts were not in vain. For with each revelation, he uncovered a piece of the puzzle, shining a light into the darkest corners of society and exposing the lies that threatened to undermine it.

As he delved deeper into his investigation, Peter encountered resistance from those who sought to silence him, to obscure the truth and maintain their grip on power. But he refused to be silenced, his voice growing stronger with each attempt to silence it.

In moments of doubt, Peter drew strength from the unwavering support of his family and the countless individuals who stood behind him. Their belief in his mission fueled his determination, propelling him forward even in the face of adversity.

And so, with courage in his heart and truth as his shield, Peter Pomerantsev continued to fight the good fight, knowing that the pursuit of truth was not just a noble endeavor—it was a fundamental necessity for the preservation of democracy and the protection of human rights. And he would not rest until justice prevailed and truth triumphed over deception.

Made in United States
North Haven, CT
18 March 2024

50139232R00024